# TO FIND HOPE

## Simple Wisdom for Those Who Grieve

### Karlene Kay Ryan

*Paulist Press*
*New York/Mahwah, N.J.*

# Acknowledgments

*Though it would be difficult to acknowledge here all those who made this book possible, I must make special mention of Meg Brookman, sharer of the creative spark, for her compassion and her keen editing sense. And to Maria L. Maggi and Kevin A. Lynch, C.S.P. at Paulist Press, for their guidance, encouragement, and support.*

Library of Congress Cataloging-in-Publication Data

Ryan, Karlene Kay, 1940–
To find hope: simple wisdom for those who grieve / Karlene Kay Ryan.
    p.   cm.
  ISBN 0-8091-3735-6  (alk. paper)
  1. Children–Death–Religious aspects–Christianity–Meditations.  2. Bereavement–Religious aspects–Christianity–Meditations.  3. Grief–Religious aspects–Christianity–Meditations.  4. Consolation.  I. Title.
BV4907.R83   1997
242´.4–dc21                                     97-15027
                                             CIP

Cover design by James F. Brisson

Cover and interior illustrations by Karlene Kay Ryan

Interior design by Kathleen Doyle

Published by Paulist Press
997 Macarthur Boulevard
Mahwah, N.J. 07430

Printed and bound in the United States of America

*This book is dedicated to the child*
*who went ahead to light the way.*

## Foreword

My son, Timothy Michael Ryan, age 19, was killed in an automobile accident on April 11, 1986.

This book explains how I found hope. It is a simply written synopsis of wisdom born from experience. My purpose in writing it is to send a message of love, to give an embrace filled with gentleness, and to offer a touch of kindness that goes beyond words to each person who has experienced the death of a child. There are, ultimately, no words to describe the feelings involved with this particular grief experience. Life is never the same as before. The people involved, especially the parents, need a great amount of support and help. There are no rules or time limits. It takes what it takes. There *is* hope for finding new strength, new meaning in your life.

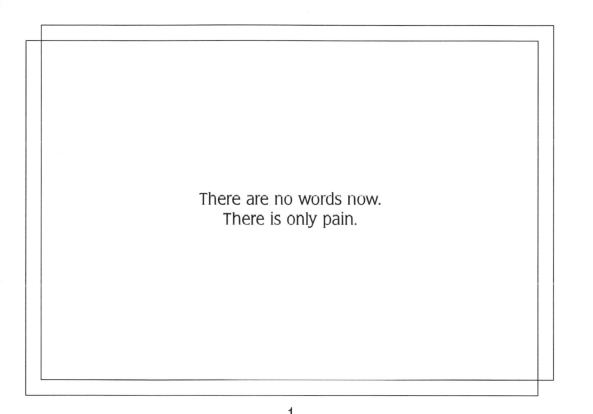

There are no words now.
There is only pain.

There are no rules for grieving.
It will take as long as it takes.
Your way of grieving is for you.
Don't try to figure it out.
Give in to it.

There are no explanations.
You are confused.
You are exhausted.
You are in shock.

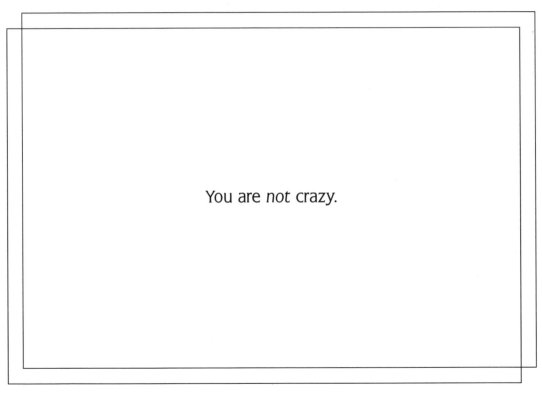

You are *not* crazy.

You are consumed with emotional pain.
It overcomes you in waves.
You can become dizzy or physically ill,
as if the world were spinning out of control.

You might be standing in a public place
and feel as though you are in a different time and space.
You might even want to scream out,
"Don't you know what has happened to me?"

You want to replay the tape of your life.
"If I had only done such and such differently."
You might beg God for another chance.

At these times, take your hands and slowly touch your face.
Give yourself gentleness and tenderness.

At these times, recognize that you are human.
Recognize that you never were in control.

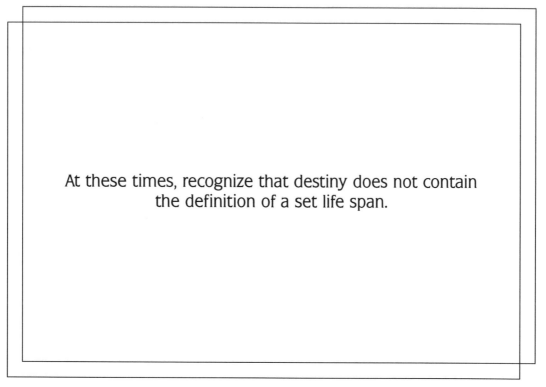

At these times, recognize that destiny does not contain
the definition of a set life span.

When you feel angry at God—tell him.
Scream it out.
Pound the pillow with anger.

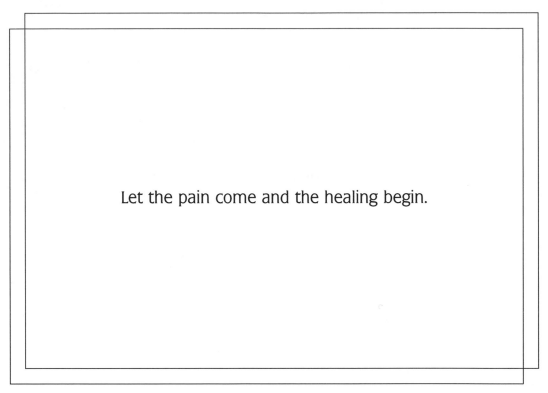

Let the pain come and the healing begin.

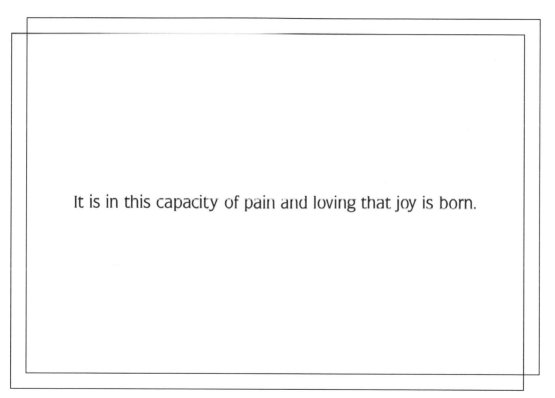

It is in this capacity of pain and loving that joy is born.

Surrender.
Learn to nurture yourself.
Give yourself rest.

Respect and give space to your spouse
and the other members of your family.

You cannot grieve for anyone else.

But you can help each other ease grief.
Touch often.
Give loving hugs.
Buy each other a teddy bear.
Cry your sorrow into its softness and rock it for comfort.

It is necessary to tell friends about your loss.
It is necessary to tell strangers.

Sometimes friends walk away and avoid you.
Try to know that those friends are fearful of pain.
But others are willing just to be there.
Reach out for this love.

Ask for help.
Ask for comfort and support at work, at church, and at home.

Allow yourself professional guidance from someone who
understands the death of a child.

Find someone who has been through a similar loss and
invite that person to be your grieving partner.
Reach out and allow someone
who knows what you are experiencing
to be kind and loving to you.

Through your vulnerability, you will learn to receive.
Through your vulnerability, you will learn to give.

Open up your whole self to God.

Surrender yourself into God's all-powerful love.
It is better with God as a part of your grief than without him.

At such a crossroads, God fills your life with extra grace.
Know grace is there.
Embrace it.

His grace will carry you and comfort you.

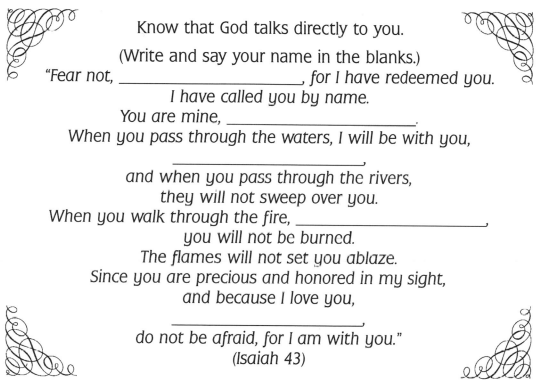

Know that God talks directly to you.

(Write and say your name in the blanks.)

"Fear not, _____, for I have redeemed you.
I have called you by name.
You are mine, _____.
When you pass through the waters, I will be with you,

_____,

and when you pass through the rivers,
they will not sweep over you.
When you walk through the fire, _____,
you will not be burned.
The flames will not set you ablaze.
Since you are precious and honored in my sight,
and because I love you,

_____,

do not be afraid, for I am with you."
(Isaiah 43)

33

The spirit of God and its life-giving energy of love
is in you.
Only this spirit will fill the chasm of your grief.
It is your strength.
It is yours for the asking.
It will heal you.

You are never separated from this spirit.
You have simply not allowed yourself to give in to this gift
because, until now, you wanted and needed someone to blame.

All the illusions of your worldly efforts are gone.
Let go. Let be. Let God.

Even though the ache is there,
you will be reaching deeper than you ever knew possible.
Through the healing,
you will come to know your real self.

This healing takes time and patience
but, in the stillness and quiet,
your mind will expand;
your eyes will see brightly;
your heart will love fully.

You will be more than you ever thought possible.
You will know what it means to live.
You will reach out and touch others with
a compassion, a humility, and a love
that you never knew before.

Nothing will ever be the same.
You will always carry sadness,
but you will know happiness.
You will begin to bring memories of your child into focus
and, at the end of the tears, you will smile.

The missing can seem unbearable.
You feel as though you will break in two.
Remember that the depth, the enormity, the intensity
of your feelings
reflect the capacity that you have for loving.

In celebration of your child's being,
buy helium balloons at each memorable date
and send them, one by one,
to that spirit-filled place where your child now lives.

Write letters to your child
about everything you did not say or do.
Everything that you dreamed.
Take the letters to your favorite place.
Read them out loud.
Cry.
Tear them up and let them blow in the wind to where they need to go.

Your child will let you know his or her spirit is near
if you stay open to hearing the messages....

You will see his face in a crowd
or turn quickly to catch a glance of
her familiar walk or gesture.
You will hear a sound in the wind
or have a bird come so close that you could touch it.

You will receive a gift that was unexpected
or flowers at an unusual time.

In the company of an old friend,
you will suddenly laugh over a family story
or be thrilled to show photographs of your child.

You will be in need of help somewhere
and a person will come to your aid
who has the same name as your child.

You will accomplish a task or set a goal
that you thought was impossible.

You will witness reconciliation and forgiveness.

You are becoming.
You will live.
And you will find that each new horizon on your journey
leads you to your child.

You will stop asking why and become fully alive again.
You will be one with God and your child.

God has received your child and he has received you.
You and your child are both in a new time and space.
You are both in a spirit-filled place of divinity and love.

There are no words or explanations or answers.
There is simply a knowing.

You have never known joy before until you have known the joy-filled feeling that comes at the end of the pain.

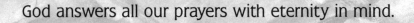

God answers all our prayers with eternity in mind.

Believe all this as real.